I've Got What It Takes!
by Jim Fay

The Love and Logic
PRESS Inc.
2207 Jackson St.
Golden, CO 80401

Library of Congress Catalog Card Number: 94-76330

ISBN 0-944634-01-X

Printed in the United States of America

Illustrated by
Paule Niedrach Botkin

Introduction

Once upon a time on the same day and in the same hospital, two babies were born. Their parents named them George and Sam.

Moments later both began working to satisfy what would be a lifelong need: feeling accepted and being noticed in a positive way.

Neither of these babies could understand the words they heard their parents say, so they used a far more powerful tool. They watched their parents very closely and learned to read nonverbal language. Soon they could notice even the most minute changes in facial expression, body tone, and voice inflection.

Over the next five years, George picked up all kinds of messages that he was capable, lovable, and valuable. His parents sent signals to him that said, "We love you the way you are, because you are you."

He also had many opportunities to make decisions about his own life. His parents often asked him questions such as, "Do you want to wear your coat today or carry it?"

They did this because they loved him and wanted the best for him.

Sam picked up messages that told him that he was not measuring up to his parents' expectations. His parents sent many messages that said, "We could have a lot more love for you if you would just do better."

His parents ordered him around often. "You get that coat on. You're not going out without it!"

They did this because they loved him and wanted the best for him.

A big day—the first day of school—finally arrived for the two boys. George entered with very few doubts about his ability, while Sam had many questions in his mind about how well he would do in school.

At school George and Sam met their teacher, Miss Hewitt. She was a loving, caring, dedicated teacher, with the same need as theirs—a need to be recognized and accepted.

She had spent her early years learning to read those same nonverbal messages. Now she was such an expert in them that she gave very little conscious thought to the nonverbal messages she picked up.

Miss Hewitt gave her class an assignment.

Confident, George quickly began and gave it his best try.

Unsure, Sam was more tentative. He stalled. A little voice in his head said, "You may not do as well as others. Watch out! You are going to be hurt."

Miss Hewitt noticed. On the conscious level she concluded that George was more capable than Sam.

On the unconscious level she realized, "George is going to satisfy my need to feel like a good teacher. Sam is not."

Miss Hewitt's behavior was molded by this second message. George, who already believed in himself, received more winks, nods, smiles, eye contact, touches, questions, and nonverbal encouragement.

At this point we no longer need to follow George's life. Barring unforeseen catastrophe, his success is assured. He knows he's got what it takes. However, we do need to follow Sam.

Sam, who was already insecure, received just the opposite treatment from Miss Hewitt—fewer nods, smiles, touches, and less eye contact.

Sam noticed. He soon picked up the message and decided, "I'm not a good student. George is the good student. The teacher likes George, but not me."

Sam was now hurting. His self-concept began to slip at a faster rate. He began to avoid pain by refusing to do assignments.

Several years went by. Sam perfected his avoidance skills. He found another way to be noticed—by being the class rebel.

His sixth grade teacher complained to the principal, "Why do I have to have kids like Sam in my class? He doesn't care about anything. Why can't I have more kids like George? He's always a good student."

She found many ways to punish Sam to try to make him change his behavior. But Sam didn't have a behavior problem; he had a self-concept problem.

When you treat a self-concept problem as a behavior problem, you make the situation worse. You actually become part of the problem, not part of the solution.

In seventh grade Sam had a very different kind of teacher. Mrs. Anderson believed that she should help each child discover and celebrate his or her strengths. She actually told the kids that they would grow up to build their life's work around their strengths instead of their weaknesses.

One day Mrs. Anderson approached Sam when he was doodling instead of doing math. She said, "Sam, I'm concerned that you are not doing your work. I do wish you would work harder in math, but those pictures you're drawing right now are beautiful. I wish you would draw one for me so that I could hang it in my home. Would you do that for me—preferably not during math class?"

He looked up and asked, "Would you like three?"

The next morning Sam came to school with three freshly drawn pictures. His teacher studied them a long time. "Oh, Sam," she said, "They're so beautiful I can't decide. Would you give me all three?"

"They're yours, Mrs. Anderson," he said. "I can always draw more."

That day Sam didn't give his teacher as much trouble as usual. As time went on, he began following her around, wanting to be close. He offered to clean blackboards, carry books, and empty the trash.

One day he told her, "You don't have to put up with these rough kids. Give me the word, and I'll teach them a good lesson after school."

Sam didn't get much better in math that year, but he was a very cooperative student.

Sam's eighth grade teacher did not appreciate his drawing. She told him, "Put that away. This is not an art class."

By this point, Sam considered himself an artist. He had graduated to colored pencils.

When his teacher spotted them one day, she held them up for his classmates as Exhibit A, broke them in half, and said, "Don't you ever let me see you with these again."

Sam changed. He started drawing in private. And he started getting even with the teacher.

Years later, as he told me this story, he said, "I got even with that old bag. I never did more than one assignment for her, and every time I got a chance, I gave her a hard time."

Sam went on to draw and draw and draw.

You've seen his art all of your life. He became one of the great cartoonists of our time.

He says he's had a great life because of one teacher who believed that we need to help children recognize their talents and build around them.

He also confesses he never did become very good at math—but that hasn't kept him from becoming a success as a cartoonist.

As a cartoonist, Sam knows that he has what it takes. Whatever their talents, we can help our children do the same.

Jim Fay

Chapter 1

Mental Videos

"Hey, Jim, come with us and try skiing this weekend," a friend says to me. I've never skied before, but I've seen it on Saturday afternoon sports specials.

And when my friend says, "Hey, Jim . . . "my self-concept immediately sends one of two movies to my mind's video screen.

The Thrill of Victory

I picture myself riding the slopes, slowly at first, and then eventually spraying snow with my parallel turns as I learn the needed mix of balance and speed.

The Agony of Defeat

I picture myself tumbling in spread-eagle somersaults, collapsing in a heap, and being dragged off on a stretcher.

My answer to my friend's invitation will be determined by which video I play. The video I play is selected by my self-concept.

Some people—who are no more athletic than others—learn to ski simply because their self-concept plays the right video. Their self-concept says, "I've got what it takes."

The right video allows some people, who are not any smarter or stronger than anyone else, to build successful businesses, earn degrees, become leaders in their field, and win competitions.

How do children learn to play the success video instead of the defeat video? It's part of a long childhood process in which children come to realize that they have what it takes. Parents can help to provide a path to that realization.

As I counsel families, I realize more and more that a good self-concept is crucial to a meaningful and useful life. That's why maintaining a child's self-concept is one of the four basic principles of Love and Logic, a philosophy I developed with my good friend, Foster W. Cline, M.D.

At the Love and Logic Institute we believe in raising children with love and logic. Love allows children to grow through their mistakes; logic allows them to live with the consequences of their choices.

Along with this book I've also written *Tickets to Success* and *Helicopters, Drill Sergeants, and Consultants*. In these companion books I focus on the first three principles of the Love and Logic process:

1. Shared Control—Parents gain control by giving away the control they don't need.

2. Shared Thinking and Decision-making—Parents provide opportunities for a child to do the greatest amount of thinking and decision-making.

3. Equal Shares of Consequences and Empathy—An absence of parental anger causes a child to think and learn from his or her mistakes.

In this third book I transport you inside children's minds to understand the fourth principle of Love and Logic parenting:

4. Maintain the Child's Self-concept—Improved self-concept leads to improved behavior and improved achievement.

High self-concept is the key to a child's success. Throughout this book you'll find the tools to help your children say, "I've got what it takes," while they hold the key to a golden future.

Using the process outlined here, parents, too, can conclude, "I've got what it takes to parent my children."

Chapter 2

Winners and Losers

People who become winners are different. They may not be smarter, but somehow they go to the top. It's as if they believe that if they keep their eyes focused ahead, their noses to the grindstone, and their feet moving, they will get somewhere.

And they do.

Howard did. And 600 of his classmates and I realized it at our ten-year high school reunion.

At our reunion, as classmates were describing their perfect jobs, homes, kids, and cars, an elegant stretch limousine arrived. Faces dropped and heads turned to see who had made it really big.

The chauffeur opened the door and Howard emerged.

"Howard!" we said. "You're wealthy—you're mega-rich. This is fantastic!"

Inside we moaned, "This can't be! Howard? Wealthy? He was a poor student. He copied from our tests, and his girlfriends wrote his papers—otherwise he wouldn't have been able to graduate."

"How did you do it?" we asked.

"It's the darndest thing," he said. "I went from one dead-end job to another, until a friend opened my eyes. He told me if I could buy a gizmo for $2 and make a few adjustments, I could turn around and sell it for $4.

"I did just that. And I sold gobs of gizmos. You know, it's amazing how much money you can make on just a two percent markup!"

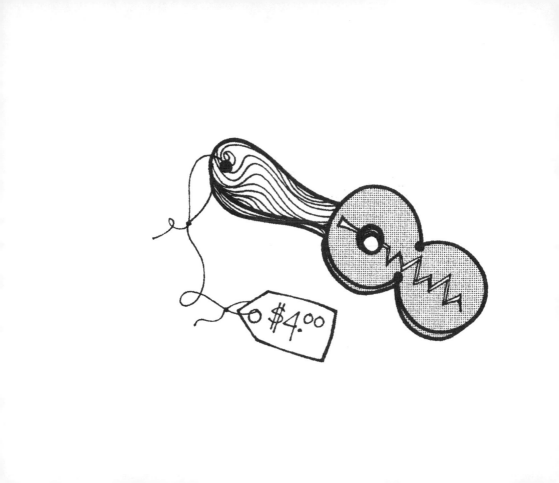

Obviously, Howard didn't get rich on his mathematical genius. But he apparently believed, "I've got what it takes. I can do it if I just keep working at it."

That belief is called a positive self-concept.

Not everyone has a positive self-concept. Many people believe, "It won't make any difference. I'm no good at things like that. There's no sense in working at it. Things will just turn out bad. Even if I try, I can't be successful."

These beliefs reflect a poor self-concept.

Our self-concept control center can be a marvelous source of encouragement or a tyrannical dictator. It is a video tape player that gives us previews of coming attractions—not just on the ski slopes, but in all aspects of life.

When a teacher says, "Students, do this assignment. You will learn, and it will be good for you," the students immediately receive their own video projections from their self-concept control centers.

Some students see themselves being successful and probably start the assignment right away. The teacher sees them as cooperative and motivated.

Other students might see a different picture that indicates, "You were never good at this. You will fail. Watch out! There's some pain on the way when people see you can't do this. It's time to go to the restroom or sharpen some pencils. No sense rushing into pain."

The teacher probably sees these students as unmotivated, uncooperative, or lazy.

These students are, in fact, just being human. They are protecting their self-concepts by avoiding activities which may remind them of their weaknesses.

A big mistake we tend to make with a child who appears unmotivated to do schoolwork is to find ways to make him do the work.

It is the child's self-concept that is the villain here, not the child.

What we should be doing instead is searching for ways to help the child develop a more positive video picture, a picture that says, "You can do it."

Chapter 3

The Self-concept Equation

Psychological research has taught us much about our self-concept and its development.

We know that our self-concept lives in our subconscious mind. Our subconscious is much like a computer. One of its functions is to store our experiences and perceptions in a memory bank.

Our memory bank is huge. It stores all of the experiences and perceptions we have ever had. These can never be taken away by surgery or by psychiatry.

Our memory is able to retrieve information and make it available to us in a split second, far faster than any computer.

Our subconscious computer has its drawbacks, though. It does not evaluate. It stores all information as fact—regardless of the reliability of that information. Faulty perceptions (imaginary events, misinformation, misinterpreted information) are all stored as fact.

Because our subconscious does not sift or evaluate, when a five-year-old believes his mother likes his brother better, subconsciously he may still believe the same at age 25. What went into his computer as perception comes out later as reality, and he says to his mother, "You never liked me. You always liked him better. You always gave him preferential treatment."

The memories and perceptions that originally entered our computer become available to us later on an unconscious basis and often influence our decision-making.

Our subconscious computer is not fooled by the words it hears. It is able to process every piece of information available, such as body language, facial expression, and tone of voice.

This multiple processing ability is the reason you don't give your name, rank, and social security number when confronted with the question, "Who do you think you are?"

At a rate of four quadrillion facts per second, your computer is processing data and asking, "What does that person really mean with those words, that tone of voice, and that body language?"

The self-concept in our subconscious computer will alter our conclusions.

In my years of research on self-concept I read more than 100 books and articles, and at the end of my study I concluded that all research and study on the subject could be reduced to one simple equation:

IC-INC=SC

IC is the I'm Capable messages account.

INC is the I'm Not Capable messages account.

SC is Self-concept.

The equation means this: The sum of all of the I'm Capable messages I have stored in memory minus the sum of all of the I'm Not Capable messages I have experienced equals my Self-concept.

Let's look at how this works in real life.

Teresa lives with encouraging parents. Every day she hears more positive than negative things about herself.

Her parents give her many choices, and they let her live with the consequences of her choices.

When she makes a wise choice, they say, "You do a great job of thinking for yourself, " or "I bet you feel good when you do such a nice job."

By the time she is twelve, her I'm Capable messages account has ten million entries, but her negative, I'm Not Capable messages account has one million.

Because her positive self-perceptions outweigh her negative ones, Teresa has a positive self-concept.

Linda, on the other hand, lives with critical parents.

They complain about her.

They tell her she is driving them crazy.

They ask, "What is the matter with you? When will you ever learn?"

By the time Linda is twelve, her I'm Capable messages account has only one million entries, and her negative I'm Not Capable messages account has ten million.

Because her negative self-perceptions outweigh her positive ones, Linda has a negative self-concept.

Obviously, Linda has a self-concept disadvantage. Her I'm Capable account needs filling.

But filling that account can be difficult, because Linda has been conditioned to hear negative assessments more easily than positive ones. Teresa has just the opposite filter. She hears positive comments about herself more easily. Filtering occurs in both cases because messages that contradict self-concept are rejected by it, while messages that support self-concept are accepted.

If I see myself as ranking at two on a ten-point scale, what does my subconscious do when a loved one says, "Hey, you're good at that!"?

My subconscious rejects the statement.

I think, "Oh, well. She loves me. She's just trying to make me feel good."

When my subconscious rejects a statement, I don't store that message in my I'm Capable account.

If, however, someone puts me down by saying, "You jerk! What's wrong with you?," I store that message.

After all, it agrees with the way I see myself.

A key, then, to a good self-concept is to begin filling that I'm Capable account bit-by-bit early in a child's life. It's easier to build a positive self-concept than to replace a negative one.

Chapter 4

Spirit Killers and Spirit Builders

S ometimes well-meaning parents can sabotage the development of a child's positive self-concept with criticism. Criticism is a spirit killer.

Each critical remark is just one more negative message for storage in the I'm Not Capable account.

I believe that there is absolutely no such thing as constructive criticism.

My plane flight from Denver to New York with John confirmed my belief.

John was distraught about his son. When he learned that I was an educator, with tears brimming behind his eyelids, he began pouring out his story.

"When my son Paul was born, I wanted more than anything for him to be happy. I knew that being happy required skills, good manners, good diction, and a good education."

"I tried my best to train him in these, but he was hardheaded, and he just wouldn't listen. I constantly had to be on his case."

"I didn't enjoy his childhood because training him was such hard work. Mealtimes I worked on his eating habits and manners. He took huge bites—he still does—and never used a napkin."

"When he talked, I so often had to remind him not to use 'ain't,' or double negatives, or street slang. If I stopped him, he would say it right, but by the next sentence he would forget."

"Nothing seemed to reach that kid. He was stubborn and hardheaded. Nothing worked—until I discovered correcting him in front of friends. That's the only time he showed any remorse or cried."

"My wife told me I criticized him too much, so I had to straighten her out, too."

"I do not criticize him. I correct him," I told her.

"I bet he still feels criticized," she said.

"She was such a limp noodle. I told her I was sick of having to do all the yelling at him."

"In elementary school—you know how it is—his teacher called us. She said, 'He has the ability. He just seems afraid to try to do assignments.'"

"Look," I told her, 'he's just a hardheaded kid who needs a teacher to take charge. I pay good taxes for you. If you can't do your job, we'll ask the principal to transfer him to a teacher who can.'"

"We finally transferred him to a private school. That was a little better, but he never was much of a student. We had to be on his back constantly."

"Junior high was a disaster. He barely slid by."

"And he spent most of his time in his room—which was fine. He was no fun anyway, always sullen and angry."

He started high school this year.

The counselor called.

He showed us Paul's notebook with morbid poems and drawings.

He said Paul needed therapy. He might be suicidal.

He said Paul wasn't stubborn, just afraid to try.

He said the reason Paul didn't do assignments was his fear that he wouldn't do them well enough.

He said . . . here a few tears escaped to John's lashes . . . He said criticism kills the spirit.

Our flight touched down in New York, and John and I parted. I sometimes wonder about him—and about Paul.

Even if John never criticizes him again, the criticism will continue. Paul has taken over the job. His father's voice runs inside his head each time he considers a new activity. It says, "You can't do it well enough. There's no sense trying."

All John wanted was for his son to be happy. But children who grow up with criticism grow up to be critical and chronically unhappy.

With his criticism, John made it almost impossible for Paul to be happy. He was a well-meaning parent who sabotaged the development of his son's self-concept through criticism.

Every critical remark was a deposit into Paul's I'm Not Capable account. These deposits will be with Paul for the rest of his life.

Want to train kids without criticism? Here's how:

Don't tell them what is wrong with what they are doing. Simply show them how to do it correctly.

"Would you like to see how I do that?," is far more effective than, "Why can't you do anything right? Do it the way I told you!"

Don't look at your child's school papers with an eye for incorrect answers. Look for the correct answers and ask your child to explain the reasons for his or her success.

Each time a child figures out reasons for success, I'm Capable messages are being deposited in his or her account. Deposits in the I'm Capable account are spirit builders, not spirit killers.

Susie's parents knew about spirit builders. Susie came from Asia as an adopted child. She joined a family who valued achievement and personal responsibility.

In a few years she had moved to the head of her class.

Her classmates asked her why she got such high grades. They thought it was because Asians usually excel at academics.

Susie said simply, "I just do my homework before I go out to play."

By her high school graduation, Susie had become valedictorian.

At her graduation one couple commented to Susie's parents about how impressed they were with Susie's academic achievements. "She must have a natural gift for school," they said.

Susie's father answered, "No, not really. Susie seems to be a pretty normal kid. But I think where she differs from a lot of other kids is that she knows we expect her to be responsible."

"When she is not, she lives with the consequences. We expect Susie to be respectful, to do her chores, and to apply herself to her schoolwork."

He added, "Susie knows where we stand. She knows that in America she has the right to life, liberty, and the pursuit of happiness—not to life, liberty, and someone else providing happiness for her. I guess she's been successful because she's busy pursuing her happiness through achievement and personal responsibility."

When Susie's father suggested her success was a result of hard work and struggle, the other parents said, "Just a moment! Doesn't that give Susie an unfair advantage? Whatever became of equal opportunity?"

Susie's father answered, "If you look at it that way, there may never be equal opportunity. As long as some people work harder than others and value achievement through struggle, they will always have an advantage. That's the value that America was founded on."

Each time Susie's parents gave her a responsibility and held her accountable, they were making I'm Capable deposits.

Susie's mother could have said, "Susie, I'll tell you how to solve that problem." Susie's subconscious would have concluded, "Mom doesn't think I can figure it out." Susie would have heard an I'm Not Capable message and made a deposit into her I'm Not Capable account.

Instead Susie's mother said, "Well, Susie, how do you think you are going to solve that?" Susie's subconscious mind concluded, "Mom knows I can think for myself." Susie heard an I'm Capable message and made a deposit into her I'm Capable account.

Susie's father could have said, "You get that coat on right now!" Susie would have concluded, "Dad thinks I'm not smart enough to know whether I'm hot or cold." Another deposit would have been made to her I'm Not Capable account.

Instead her father said, "Would you rather wear your coat or carry it?" Susie concluded, "Dad trusts me to know what's best for me." Another I'm Capable deposit was made into that account.

Some parents are different from Susie's. They try to protect their children from struggle.

They say, "I don't want my children to have to work night and day like I did. I want them to have a better life and all the things I never had."

But allowing children to struggle to succeed allows them to make deposits into their I'm Capable account. It allows them to conclude:

I can think for myself.

I can solve my own problems.

I have healthy control over my life.

I can achieve if I'm willing to put forth effort.

Because many parents protect their children from struggle, fewer and fewer students in our public schools appear to be willing to accept working hard as a necessary part of learning. Teachers, instead, are working harder and harder to find new ways to motivate students who often believe that the teachers are being mean by asking them to put forth effort.

Schools are criticized because students are not achieving as well as in the past. However, changing the schools will not solve this problem. Our schools will be plagued with underachieving students until our entire society changes its messages about the value of struggle.

That's the bad news.

The good news is that your child can stand out and have a real advantage, if you allow him or her to struggle. When they put forth this effort, children also learn to be responsible. When teachers challenge them to achieve, these kids think, "That's no big deal. I get what I want through working hard. I've got what it takes!"

Chapter 5

How to Provide the I'm Capable Advantage

At home and at school children can grow up believing they have what it takes. They can make deposits into their I'm Capable accounts day-by-day with a few basic I'm Capable Builders.

I'm Capable Builder #1
Require Chores

Regardless of what your kids say about chores being unfair and about none of their friends having to do chores, children need to contribute to the welfare of the family. It is reasonable to expect children as young as six to have a minimum of twenty minutes of chores to do each day.

Children can learn to do their chores without a battle. Here's how:

Spend a couple of weeks listing all the jobs that have to be done in order for your family to survive. Keep this list on the refrigerator and each time you think of another one of the family jobs, add it to the list.

The list should also include all the jobs parents usually do—earning money, balancing the checkbook, paying bills, driving the car, shopping, cooking food, making beds, washing clothes, etc.

Invite your children to list the things they need parents to do for them—driving them to soccer practice, ironing and mending clothes, picking them up from the mall, taking care of pets, etc.

Have a family meeting to divide the jobs. Obviously, most kids won't choose to go to work every day or to pay the bills, and most aren't old enough to play chauffeur, so you will probably have to offer to do those chores. Out of the remaining jobs, the kids may select those they would most like to do. (If they don't like any, they may choose the ones they hate the least.)

It's wise not to assign jobs so that kids have to depend on each other or do them together. This combination can lead to unnecessary arguments.

One technique for getting chores done is to say, "There is no hurry each day to do your choices. Just be sure they are done by the end of the day."

Do not remind them about their chores. If the jobs are not done by the end of the day, say nothing. Let the kids go to bed. Let them sleep 30-45 minutes.

Then wake them up—gently, but persistently. Remind them that the end of the day is near and they need to finish their work. Don't take "no" for an answer!

When the chore is completed, you can say, "There! The day is complete. I'm glad we can go to sleep knowing that the day's work is done."

When children have chores, their I'm Capable accounts can grow faster than their I'm Not Capable accounts.

Children who feel a sense of contribution and success through effort have an advantage over other children.

I'm Capable Builder #2
Provide Matching Funds

Bombarded by media ads, kids have developed a high need for material things. As parents we have two temptations.

We are tempted to give them all we can as a show of love. This unconditional giving robs children of the opportunity to struggle. When children have not learned to work toward goals, they are then at risk for underachievement in school. They don't realize that achievement requires effort.

We are also tempted to say, "You don't need those things." This negative response is also ineffective. Even if we succeed in preventing the purchase, we rob our children of the chance to work hard to get the things they want.

We have a third choice.

When children ask us to buy something, we can implement a matching funds policy.

Tommy may announce, "I just have to have those basketball shoes. All the other kids have them. They're only $125."

Instead of either readily shelling out the $125 or refusing his request, we can respond with, "If it's that important to you, you ought to have them. I think you'd look like a pro in them. I can contribute $35. As soon as you earn the rest, we can buy the shoes."

Tommy may put up a fight. "That's not fair. The other kids' parents buy them."

"I know. It can be rough living on a tight budget. Let me know when you're ready for the $35."

Tommy will wear those new shoes with greater pride once he has struggled to earn them.

Your value system can dictate the amount you provide each time. Sometimes you may contribute ten percent, sometimes seventy-five percent, and sometimes ninety percent. (An occasional outright gift is okay, too.)

It's your money. You get to decide.

However, it's important to remember that children who earn what they get gradually learn self-respect, resourcefulness, the value of money, and—most importantly—that problems are solved through struggle.

These children have an advantage. They are making deposits in their I'm Capable accounts faster than into their I'm Not Capable accounts.

I'm Capable Builder #3
Offer Multiple Solutions

Children who find their own solutions to problems have more self-respect than those who don't.

Many parents are tempted to run interference for children. It is hard on them to see their children having problems. However, parents who frequently solve their children's problems raise kids who are emotionally crippled. These children come to believe their parents' unstated message, "You can't solve your own problems."

It feels natural for these kids to give up when they have a problem. They look helplessly at their parents and moan, "I can't do it."

It feels even more natural for these parents to say, "Oh, no! If I don't take over, my child will never do it for himself."

These parents soon find themselves sucked into their kids' problems, suggesting solution after solution. The sad part is that these kids never seem to like their parents' suggestions.

The next time your child comes to you with a problem, try something different. Listen with empathy and follow with a question. "It sounds like that is really bothering you. What do you think you are going to do?"

Most kids will say, "I don't know."

Then say, "That's sad not to know. Would you like to hear what some other kids have tried?

If the youngster says, "Yes," and you can't readily come up with some good and bad examples, tell your child that you will give it some thought and get back to him or her.

This will give you a chance to think it out or to call a friend to help you make up a list of suggestions. There is no advantage to giving an immediate solution. The importance of this process is to provide some choices for the child instead of just one solution.

When you have some possible solutions, present them to the child one at a time and after each one ask the child to evaluate the solution.

If, for example, your son has a problem not getting along with a few neighbor children, you could say, "Some kids get an army of other kids and threaten the kids they are having problems with. How do you think that would work out?"

I watched a parent try this technique once. She couldn't think of any good solutions, so she suggested four bad ones and asked each time, "How would that work?"

Finally her daughter said, "Those ideas aren't any good. I think I'll just try to talk it out with her."

Her mother remarked, "It was great to see Sally learning to think for herself!"

Children who learn that they can solve their own problems have an advantage over others. Their I'm Capable accounts grow to outweigh their I'm Not Capable accounts.

I'm Capable Builder #4
Ask for Explanations of Success

Our natural tendency as parents is to watch for our children's mistakes and failures and then instruct them about what went wrong. Such instruction makes deposits into the wrong account—the I'm Not Capable account.

Instead, watch for a youngster to be successful, and say, "I bet that feels great! You must really feel proud. Why do you think you were able to do that?"

Most kids will respond, "I don't know." That response gives you a chance to say, "Well, you either tried hard or you are getting smarter. Which do you think it is?"

Asking for explanations of success is one of the most powerful and effective techniques that exists for building positive self-concept.

Whichever explanation a child chooses, a powerful deposit is made into his or her I'm Capable account.

I'm Capable Builder #5
Provide an Environment for School Success

School takes up a huge chunk of childhood, and provides many opportunities for building up I'm Capable accounts.

Kids who learn that their education is their education take more interest in it. They are more willing to struggle to learn. When they succeed—through their own efforts—their I'm Capable accounts build faster than their I'm Not Capable accounts.

They have an advantage.

It's important to remember that parents can't teach for teachers and teachers can't do the parenting.

Instead a parent can provide opportunities so that a child's school experiences add to his or her I'm Capable account.

Here's how:

1. Show the same amount of love for your children regardless of their success in school. Tell your children that you will love them regardless of their grades or the number of years it takes to complete each grade.

If your child has a hard time at school, at the end of the school day he or she needs to get away from it for a while. Help your child find after-school activities where he or she can feel successful.

Asking a teacher to give more homework to a child who struggles during the day with school work is like asking an adult who has a stressful job to do more of the same when he or she gets home from work.

2. Spend some time each day talking with excitement about your work and your day. Children naturally want to imitate and will soon begin to talk about school and their day. Once a week ask your children to teach you something they learned at school.

3. Take turns reading to each other every day.

4. Direct your children toward activities that restore their spirits. Encourage them to become involved in and to try many different activities as a way of discovering interests and talents. Remind them that they will build their careers around their talents and strengths, not their weaknesses.

5. Provide a time and place for homework, and let your children know that they are expected to study. Allow them to study either by writing the assignments or thinking hard about them for a reasonable amount of time. If they decide to study

by thinking, have them think of a plan for explaining this decision to their teacher.

6. Have your children bring home their school papers, and look for the right answers instead of the wrong ones. DON'T CORRECT THE WRONG ANSWERS .Leave this for the teacher. Instead, ask your children to explain how they got the right answers. If they don't know, give them three choices:

You cheated?

You tried hard?

You're getting smarter in that subject?

When children conclude that their right answers were from hard work or intellectual development, they make additional deposits into their I'm Capable accounts.

7. Don't pay for good grades or punish for bad ones. Simply be excited about the good ones, and sad for your children about the bad ones.

I have often talked with children who are not doing well in school and asked this question: "Who do you think worries the most about your grades, you or your parents?"

I always get the same answer: "My parents."

As long as children have others who will worry about their problems, they don't worry about them. Children think, "Since my parents have that worry well in hand, there's no sense in both of us worrying about it."

Parents who offer to pay for good grades or who punish for bad ones take over too much of the worry about their children's grades. And they raise the odds that their children will see achievement as something being forced rather than offered.

Once a youngster sees grades as part of a power struggle, the issue is no longer about the value of a good education but about who is going to win. As long as a child has two choices—to succeed or not to succeed—he or she still has a good chance of success.

However, a child in a power struggle sees only one choice: winning the power struggle.

Providing the I'm Capable advantage doesn't happen instantly. The I'm Capable account increases day-by-day as we use I'm Capable Builders. The I'm Capable account grows as we:

Require chores

Provide matching funds

Offer multiple solutions

Ask for explanations of success

Provide an environment for school success

With this environment, children will grow up believing they've got what it takes.

Conclusion

Barry Neil Kauffman, a leading psychologist, says, "The way to change a person's behavior is to first change the way he sees the world." He says people do the very best they can considering the way they see themselves and the world.

Our behavior is determined by our self-concept. And we have seen that our self-concept is a balance of I'm Capable and I'm Not Capable messages.

Building an I'm Capable account takes time. Shifting the balance from the I'm Not Capable side to the I'm Capable side takes even longer. But with day-by-day investment in their lives, we can shift the balance and the results can be amazing.

A twelve-year-old from Kansas now has what it takes. He is much better prepared for the adult world he will soon face. His dad put "Love and Logic" to work, allowing him to solve his own problems related to his arrest for shoplifting.

This father said a million thoughts ran through his mind as he drove to pick up his son Bobby. He considered ranting, raving, and rescuing.

Then he decided to build Bobby's I'm Capable account instead, using Love and Logic Principles, and letting the consequences be the bad guy.

Dad met a very sheepish child at the detention center. "Don't be mad, Dad. I'm sorry. I'll never do anything this stupid again."

He replied, "I'm not mad, son, but I do feel sad about what you will have to go through. I guess you know that you will have to appear in court, and I don't know what the judge will do. I hope that you are strong enough for this."

He explained to Bobby that he would need legal representation, and gave him the names of some lawyers to call.

Bobby gulped, took the list of names, and started dialing.

Several phone calls later he told his Dad, "The cheapest lawyer I can find will charge $600. That's a rip-off!"

"Professional help is often expensive," said his father. "Maybe I can help. In this state, parents can represent their children in court. I'm not a lawyer, so I could do it for half price. Maybe you want to think that over awhile and let me know."

Bobby's thinking lasted four seconds. "I want you to represent me, but I don't have $300. Will you loan me the money?"

Dad was willing to make a loan—with a legal promissory note registered in the Secretary of State's office. Dad took Bobby to an office supply store to purchase a legal promissory note form. They filled it out together and Bobby signed it. Then Bobby filed a copy at the Secretary of State's office.

Father and son finally appeared before the judge in juvenile court. "Young man, are you represented by legal counsel?" asked the judge.

"Yes, sir," said Bobby. He explained about his father's bargain price, the promissory note, and the trip to the Secretary of State.

"How does your client plead in this matter?" asked the judge.

Dad said, "My client is pleading guilty, Your Honor."

"Fine," said the judge. "Do you have anything to say before I rule?"

"Yes, Your Honor," offered Dad. "Bobby is a good boy. He has never been in trouble before. He does his chores and works hard at school. He admits he made a big mistake and does not plan to repeat this behavior. He is requesting that you consider a deferred judgment. He is even suggesting that the period of time be twelve months instead of the regular six-month deferred judgment, so he can prove to the court he can stay out of trouble for that period of time."

The judge struck his gavel and said, "So ordered. Stay out of trouble, young man. Now stand down!"

Father and son left the courtroom together and headed for the car in silence. As they settled into their seats for the trip home, Bobby looked at his father and said, "You know what, Dad? Back there you were awesome!"

Bobby's dad was indeed awesome. He had given Bobby an opportunity to build his I'm Capable account by working hard, providing funding, and making choices. Bobby took responsibility for his actions, and he learned to believe in himself.

Children who believe in themselves can even become adults who, like Howard, make an enormous profit on a two percent markup!

More importantly, their subconscious computers will be friendly encouragers instead of tyrannical dictators.

And the internal videos they play will be broadcasts of victory, not defeat.

When their I'm Capable accounts have grown day by day, children become adults who know at their core, "I've got what it takes."

It will show in how they behave.

They may even take up skiing.

Let's meet at the slopes.